Pip! Zip! Hatch! Love!

A Complete Kid's Guide To Keeping Chickens

By Susanne Blumer

Pip! Zip! Hatch! Love!

A Complete Kid's Guide To Keeping Chickens

Susanne Blumer

This book is dedicated to my husband Cole who only wanted land and ended up with 500 chickens and a lot of hard work. You have always been the fulfiller of my dreams… even the crazy ones. Thank you!

And to my children, Colin & Annaliese, who started on this chicken adventure with me and supported their mom through it all. Thank you for collecting so many eggs through the years, for not laughing too hard when I said I needed more chickens, and for loving them so much. You both rock!

And to all the chickens who touched my heart, thank you. If only you could read.

ISBN 978-0-9966164-0-9
Printed in the United States of America

First Printing, 2015

chickadillypress.com

Why Chickens And Not A Hamster?

There are so many wonderful reasons to raise chickens.

- They give you eggs. Yum! And eggs are good for you too!
- They have funny personalities and will make you laugh.
- Keeping chickens is a wonderful way to learn to care for a pet.
- Chickens come in so many different colors, shapes and sizes. You can pick the perfect one for you!
- They give you eggs.... Wait....We already said that, didn't we? That's okay. It's a great reason! How many people have a pet that makes them breakfast? Hamsters don't. At least, I think they don't.

So what's your reason? More than one? Let's take a closer look at how to get your flock started.

Where Do I Get Chickens Anyway?

There are several ways to get your first chickens. Pick the one that works best for you and your family.

- You can buy chicks from a local breeder, a friend or at a local feed store (stores normally stock chicks during the spring). Raising your flock up from chicks will help you get to know them from teeny tiny babies. If you hold them a lot while they are young, your chickens can turn out to be very friendly when they are older. Some will even follow you around and want you to pick them up!

- You can order chicks from a hatchery or a breeder somewhere in the United States. Did you know the regular old post office will deliver your live chicks right to your door? They do! And they are normally just one-day old! Hatcheries are a wonderful source for all kinds of chickens. You can look through their catalog and pick out exactly what you want!

- You might be able to find someone in your area that is selling some of their chickens. Have one of your parents help you look on the internet. They will probably know some good places to search.

- A super exciting way to start your flock is to buy hatching eggs from someone in your area (or even in another state) and put them in an incubator to hatch. We will talk all about hatching in a little while, but I promise you it is a lot of fun. You will learn so much while doing it! Unless you have a mama chicken that wants to hatch some babies for you (and you probably don't since you are reading this book about how to raise chickens!), you will need to talk to your parents about buying an incubator. Or you could save up your allowance for one. There are some really good incubators that are not too expensive and will work perfectly for hatching out a small flock of chickens. Try it!

- You could put an egg under your pillow and hope the Chick Fairy comes by during the night and leaves you some baby chicks in place of the egg. I don't really recommend this way though. I've tried it and not only did it not work, I smashed the egg during the night and had a big mess to clean up in the morning. Not Fun!

> Hopefully this gives you some good ideas of where to get your first chicks or chickens. Now we need to make sure we pick the perfect breed of chicken for you!

Picking The Perfect Breed

Did you know there are hundreds of different chicken breeds? There are! A **breed** is a certain kind of chicken.

Start by deciding what kind of chicken you want. Do you want a breed that lays a lot of eggs? Do you want really big eggs? Maybe colored eggs? Cute chickens?

Would you rather have a little, fluffy chicken that you could hold all the time? Maybe you want a breed that is really unusual looking like the Buff Polish in this picture.

No matter what you want, there is a chicken breed for you!

Some breeds have more than one size. Everything is basically the same except how big the adult bird will be and the size egg they lay.

Bantams are the small version of the breed.

Standards are the large version of the breed.

Bantams lay smaller eggs. Standards will lay larger eggs. Makes sense, right? Some people think bantams are a breed, but they're not. It's just a size. Now you know!

Some breeds of chickens lay colored eggs. Blue, green, dark brown, pink, peach. So many different colors!

But only the outside is different. They look like regular old eggs on the inside. And taste the same.

Here are some examples: **Ameraucanas** lay blue eggs.

Marans lay very dark brown eggs. **Olive Eggers** lay... olive colored eggs! And there are others too. Most breeds though lay white or light brown eggs.

Whatever color egg your hen lays, she will always lay that color. It doesn't change.

If you want a hen that lays colored eggs, find a good book at the library or book store that talks about all the different breeds of chickens and the color egg they lay. Or just do some research on the internet.

If you plan ahead, you can get a variety of colors, and then you won't have to dye eggs at Easter! You can just go out and get them from the coop. Pretty cool!

Parts Of A Chicken

The comb (the red spikes) comes in many shapes and sizes. This one is a single comb.

These long feathers around the neck are the hackles. Roosters usually have longer ones than hens.

The wattles hang underneath the beak. To the left of those are the ear lobes.

This is the tail and it come in many different styles and lengths.

These long feathers in front of the tail are the saddle feathers. Long saddle feathers almost always mean a rooster!

The legs can come in several colors. The sharp part on the back is the spur. Chickens have long toe nails that sometimes need to be trimmed!

9

All About Roosters

Roosters are always boys. A young male is called a **cockerel**. When he reaches a year old, he is called a **rooster** or a **cock**.

Whether or not you have a rooster or two is up to you. You do not need a rooster to have eggs. Your hens will lay eggs either way.

A lot of people think roosters are mean, but most breeds have very nice roosters. If you ever do end up with a not-very-nice rooster, give him away. It's possible to train him to be nice, but it normally isn't worth the trouble.

It's much easier to just get a sweet rooster. Much easier!

So why would you want a rooster anyway?

Well, they **crow**… all the time. Roosters do not just crow first thing in the morning. They crow when they are happy or to say hi. They crow when they are showing off for the ladies. They just like to crow. Cockle Doodle Do all day long! And every rooster has his own special crow. If you have more than one, you will learn who is crowing just by listening!

If you live somewhere that doesn't allow noisy crowing chickens, a rooster is probably not a good idea. But if you live out in the country and like to hear a rooster crowing, then get one!

They have other really great qualities too.

For starters, roosters are always the fanciest chickens. Hens are more drab and plain looking so that **predators** won't see them. The roosters have all the beautiful feathers and colors, and they know it too!

Roosters spend most of their day looking after their flock. They scan the sky for danger and will alert the flock if they see something. They find treats for their hens and call them over to enjoy them. Roosters also protect their flocks from harm and will go get any hen that wanders too far away from the rest of the group.

 So what do you think? Will you have one?

All About Hens

Hens are the girls of the chicken world. A young female is called a **pullet**. Once she is a year old, she is called a **hen**. Hens lay all the eggs. If you want to have chicks from the eggs, you will need a rooster. If you just want eggs, roosters are optional. Poor guys!

Pullets start laying eggs around six months old. Some breeds lay earlier, and some lay later. But usually around the time they are 24 weeks old, you will starting getting eggs. It's so exciting to collect your first egg!

Most of the year, you can expect an egg about every 26 hours. Hens need a certain number of daylight hours to lay an egg (usually around 15 hours). So in the winter when it gets dark really early, you might get fewer eggs than in the summer when it stays light longer.

If you want to keep your girls laying all year, you can put a light in the coop and put it on a timer. That makes the hen think it's daylight when it's not!

About once a year, chickens go through a **molt**. A molt is when the chicken (both boys and girls) lose a lot of their feathers and get new and improved ones. Don't be scared if you start seeing a bunch of feathers lying around the coop. Your chickens are probably just molting! They will look much fancier once their new feathers come in. Hens usually stop laying eggs while they are molting. The whole molt can take a few weeks or a few months depending on the breed.

Did you know that when hens lay eggs they sing a song? It's called the **egg song** and sounds a little like this:

Bawk Bawk Bawk Bawk BA GAWK!!!

If you start hearing that, your hens are getting ready to lay an egg! Sometimes they sing it right after they lay an egg. And even roosters join in the act! Roosters hate being left out of a good song.

Many times a pullet will start practicing the egg song when she is close to the time to start laying her eggs. That can happen for a day or two so if you hear her singing, start looking for her first egg!

Hens lay their eggs in a **nest box** like the one here. A nest box can be an actual wooden box or anything that has enough room for a hen to get in, move around, and lay her egg. She will need to feel protected in her nest box, especially if she is sitting on eggs to hatch.

A milk crate makes a perfect nest box. So does a small plastic bin. Be imaginative!

Make sure you put something in the bottom of the nest box like hay, pine shavings or shredded newspaper. But no cedar! Cedar is harmful to chickens.

A nice cozy cushion in the nest box will make her happy and help keep the eggs safe. And help keep them clean too!

One day you will go in to collect eggs and find four chickens crammed into one nest box. I don't know why they do this, but it happens all the time! And every other nest box will be empty. Chickens are a mystery sometimes!

Which came first... the chicken or the egg? See? A mystery!

Why Does My Hen Sit In The Nest Box All Day?

If you notice your hen staying in her nest box all day and never coming out, you probably have a **broody** hen.

Sometimes hens decide they want to hatch out chicks and will try to sit on eggs any chance they get.

Most of the time you will want to collect the eggs under her. Be careful when you reach in there though! Those hens can be very protective! Peck Peck! Try gently lifting her up with a stick and grabbing the eggs fast. Works for me every time!

If you have a rooster and want chicks, you can let her sit on the eggs. After 21 days, they should hatch. You will learn all about hatching soon! Most hens are wonderful mommas and will raise their chicks naturally. You will have a lot of fun watching her teach them new things and chasing after them when they run off!

If you have a hen hatch eggs and then not take care of her chicks, bring them into the house and raise them in the **brooder**. Some hens only like to hatch the chicks and will ignore them or worse.

The best way to stop a hen from being broody is to move her to a new location for a few days. Most of the time, a hen will forget about being broody, and you can move her back with the rest of the flock. Some hens stay broody forever. Forever!

Hens rarely lay eggs when they are broody so if you want eggs from her, it's a good idea to try to break her broodiness… if you can!

Certain breeds are known to be more broody than others. If you think you might like to raise chicks that way, invest in a few hens that have the potential to be broody. Silkies are notorious for being broody. Not only are they the most adorable chickens in the world, they will raise just about anything as their own. Even ducks.

This is a white silkie hen. You want one now, don't you?

What Do Chickens Do All Day?

Great question! Chickens stay quite busy most of the day. Here are some of their favorite activities:

- They spend a lot of time scratching the ground looking for bugs and other delicious goodies. Chickens love to scratch!

- They take **dirt baths**. To keep clean, chickens will find (or create) a shallow hole of dirt and lie down in it. They will move all around, flapping their wings, and use the dirt to bathe. Sometimes they just lay there, not moving, and you will find yourself running over there to save your favorite hen from certain death! No worries though. Chickens love dirt baths and you will be happy knowing they are staying clean.

- Chickens love to sun bathe! They really do! They love to find a sunny spot, lie down and lift their wings. Silly chickens.
- One thing they absolutely love to do (which makes me crazy) is tear up flower beds and gardens. Do NOT tell your parents this if they love to garden! Show a chicken a beautiful bed of flowers, and it will head right to it and scratch the whole thing to bits. They can be quite naughty.

- Your chickens will not fly off when you're not looking. Chickens like to stay near home where they know it is safe. And when it starts to get dark, they will put themselves to bed!

- Chickens love to eat snacks! They love all kinds of snacks… watermelon, salad, scrambled eggs, pasta. Throw a few grapes to your chickens and you will spend a good five minutes laughing your head off as they try to play Keep Away. Chickens can have most foods as snacks except raw potato peels and citrus fruit. Stay away from those as they are dangerous to chickens.

Did you know that you don't need to put your eggs in the refrigerator after you collect them? Eggs have a natural protective coating on them and as long as they are not washed, they do not need to be refrigerated. Isn't that interesting?

Eggciting & Unusual Chicken Facts

Did you know....

- Chickens close their eyes from the bottom? Weird, huh?
- Chickens can distinguish between over 100 different faces. They are so smart!
- Chickens dream and also have full-color vision.
- Mother hens talk to their chicks while they are still in the egg!
- A hen sitting on eggs will turn it about 50 times a day. That's dedication!
- Chickens have more bones in their necks than giraffes.
- Chickens can't taste sweetness but they can taste saltiness.
- Chickens don't pee. It's mixed in with their poop.
- Chickens definitely have a "pecking order" and will recognize the head chicken. And it's not always the rooster!
- Hens can crow! It's rare, but they can!
- Chickens have more than 30 different types of call for threats.
- There are more chickens on earth than humans!
- The chicken is the closest living relative to the Tyrannosaurus Rex. It's true! Look it up!
- Chickens can live to be to 20 years old.

Aren't chickens fascinating? They also have distinct personalities and you will enjoy getting to know your individual chickens, what they like, and how they act.

Hatching 1-2-3

Let's talk about **hatching** chicks. I have probably hatched out 3000 chicks in the last ten years. That's a lot of chicks, isn't it?

Incubating and hatching chicks is very educational and exciting but can also be frustrating. Not every hatch will be a good one, so if you decide to try it, just know that you might have some disappointments. But it's so worth it! This is a lot of information but try not to get overwhelmed. Once you start, the whole process is not hard!

I'm going to tell you everything you need to know to have the best chance at a successful hatch. So let's get started.

The first thing you will need is an **incubator**. Styrofoam incubators like this one are easy to use, work well and don't cost a ton of money. Most have a viewing window on the top so you can see what is going on in there! You will love that feature! We call that BatorVision!

BatorVision will keep you occupied for hours and hours. Your parents will be very happy you are not playing video games.

There are so many different kinds of incubators to choose from and in all different price ranges. I have one incubator that holds

300 eggs! Some people make their own incubator. Do some research and choose what is best for you. You won't need anything too fancy to start.

Make sure you get an incubator with an **egg turner** and an automatic fan. The egg turner will make your life much easier during the incubation time! Just trust me on this.

When you get your fertilized hatching eggs, let them rest at room temperature for about 24 hours and please make sure they are big side up. That is where the **air sac** is, and it's important that the egg rest that way.

While you are waiting for the eggs to come to room temperature, get your incubator ready. Make sure to read the instructions that come with your incubator to be sure you have the proper **temperature** and **humidity**. Each one is a little different.

On average, you will want your incubator's temperature to be at 99.5 degrees and the humidity to be around 45%. If your incubator does not have a built-in **thermometer** and/or **hygrometer** (that's a fancy name for the thing that measures humidity), you will need to put a small thermometer and hygrometer in your incubator. It can take several hours for the temperature and humidity to come up and regulate, so go ahead and get that started.

Once your eggs are at room temperature, you can put the eggs in! Some incubators come with trays or some other kind of equipment to keep your eggs from wobbling around. If not, a cardboard egg container works great! Just cut off the top. Gently put your eggs in big side up. You might want to mark the date you are starting on the top of the egg so you remember. But do it in pencil and not pen. Ink can leak through the egg and you don't want that!

The incubation time for chicken eggs is 21 days. The first 18 days are called the **incubation period**. The last three days are called **lockdown**, and that's where it gets exciting!

During the incubation period (or the boring period as I call it!), you must keep the temperature and humidity steady. Some incubators will require you to add water yourself, and some do it for you. Just make sure to check on everything a few times a day!

The eggs will need to be turned a few times each day while the chick grows inside. If you have an egg turner (please get one!), that will do it for you. If you don't, you will have to remember to do that by hand.

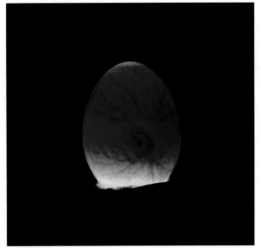

Candling involves looking into the egg with a bright light to see what's going on in there. As the chick develops, the air pocket will get smaller and the egg will fill with the chick. Many people candle at 7 days, 14 days and just prior to lockdown.

We have a little piece of cardboard with a hole cut out to hold the egg. Then we use a very strong light in a dark room to candle the eggs. It's definitely not an exact science, and the dark-shelled eggs are hard to candle. But with a little practice, you'll get the hang of what you're looking for and what a developing chick looks like. You will be amazed at everything going on in there! You don't have to candle your eggs, but it's fun!

Finally day 18 arrives, and it's time for **lockdown!** This is the period when the chick will hatch. YAY! It's very, very important to leave the eggs alone once you put them in lockdown. Humidity must be raised to 65-70% or to whatever your incubator manufacturer recommends. You remove the turner and lay the eggs on their side in the incubator. Some people use egg cartons to hold the eggs. The incubator needs to stay closed during lockdown to preserve the temperature and humidity. It is dangerous to the chicks if the humidity drops, so just leave it alone!

So remember… NO OPENING THE INCUBATOR DURING LOCKDOWN! Say it with me. Good job.

Is this what you think the chick will look like when it hatches?

Read on and let's find out.

Hint: It doesn't!

At some point during the next few days, you hope to see a **pip**. A pip is a little, itty bitty break on the egg. The chick uses its **egg tooth** to break through the shell.

That little hole is a pip. When you see that, your chick is starting to hatch! Woo hoo!

Some chicks pip and then bust on out. Some chicks pip and then take a little longer.

Be patient! You might also see the egg rocking back and forth or hear little chirping coming from an egg. Don't you wonder what's going on in there?

After the pip comes the **zip**. The chick will use its egg tooth again to break the shell all the way around. It looks like the egg is being unzipped. After that happens, it's usually fairly easy for the chick to push out of

the shell. If you see an egg zipping, keep watch! Generally the chick hatches quickly at that point.

Now I warn you…. **Chicks are not pretty when they hatch**. They look like little aliens! They come out wet, maybe a little bloody, and very weak. Sometimes part of the egg is stuck to them, and they'll flop around for a few hours, dragging the shell behind them.

They also sleep a lot and get stuck on their back at which point you'll be convinced they've died. Don't worry! Eventually they

begin to dry off and start to look like something you want to keep.

I did warn you, right?

The good news is that in a few hours your little chick will start to look all dry and fluffy.

Promise!

Chicks ingest (eat) the yolk shortly before hatching. This feeds them so they can be left in the incubator for up to three days while the rest of the eggs hatch.

You will be tempted to reach in very quickly and take one or two out. So tempted! But don't do it. The chick is perfectly warm and safe in there and opening the incubator can risk the other eggs.

Now for the bad part of incubating... Not all eggs will hatch. That's just the way it is. This happens for a variety of reasons and most of the time you won't know what they are. Please don't expect 100% of the eggs to hatch. Even your own eggs. On a hatch of eggs you get in the mail, even a 50% hatch is considered a success.

If it is day 22 and no one else has pipped or seems to be ready to hatch, take your chicks out and throw the unhatched eggs away. It's okay if some of your chicks haven't been in there three days. As long as they are dry, gently take them out and move on to brooding!

So I Have The Chicks, Now What?

Whether you buy chicks locally, hatch them or receive them in the mail, once you bring them home they will need a warm, dry, safe place to spend a few weeks. This first home is called a **brooder**.

A brooder can be all sorts of things: a big plastic bin, a cardboard box, even a bathtub! You want something that is open on the top but has high enough sides that the chicks cannot jump out. And believe me, they will be jumping out before you know it!

It also needs to be big enough to give your chicks room to move around and space to hold a feeder and waterer. Make sure you have your brooder completely ready **before** your chicks arrive or hatch

Your brooder will need something in the bottom of it for the chicks to walk around on. Some people start out with a few layers of paper towels. After a couple of days, they switch over to pine shavings. You can also start out with pine shavings right away.

You can buy pine shavings at your local feed store or farm supply company. Do not use any cedar products near chickens. Cedar is very dangerous to poultry. And don't use newspapers. Too slippery for chicks! You don't want them ice skating!

If you decide to go with shavings, put a shallow layer (1-2 inches) in the bottom of the brooder. Keep the brooder somewhere dry, safe from other animals, and away from drafts. You don't want your cats or dogs to be able to get to the chicks! You can put it in a room with the door closed, a basement or a garage.

Your new chicks will need food, water and warmth while they are in the brooder.

This is an example of a chick **waterer**. When you put your chicks in the brooder, very GENTLY dip just the tip of their beak in the water so they know what it is. They will take it from there. They learn fast!

Make sure they always have fresh, clean water. It's a good idea to put a few marbles or rocks in the dish. Chicks can sometimes fall into their water dish. The marbles/rocks will help keep them safe.

Don't be surprised if your chicks kick half of their shavings into the water. They just do. Keep their waterer clean the best you can!

Your new little flock will need a special kind of food when they start out. A medicated **chick starter** is perfect at the beginning. They should stay on this for 6-8 weeks.

As they get older, you will change to a **grower feed** until they are 17 weeks old and then to a **layer feed** to prepare them to start laying eggs. Each feed has a different make up of protein and nutrients.

Buy a **chick feeder** from your local pet or farm supply store. There are several different varieties. No matter what kind you pick, your little ones will kick the food out all over the brooder. They are messy but so cute!

When older, your chickens will also need **grit**. Grit is a mixture of small stones or pebbles that help them digest their food. You can buy it where you get your feed. Start grit once they are eating something other than feed. You can also feed them **scratch** which is a grain supplement that they love! These are in addition to their feed.

Heat is also an important part of raising your chicks. They need to be kept warm. A 250-watt **heat lamp** is perfect. Red bulbs are preferred to white.

At the very beginning, you want to keep the temperature in the brooder around 95-100 degrees. Put a little thermometer in the brooder so you can check the temperature.

A parent probably will need to help you with the heat lamp. The lamp needs to be very, very secure. You don't want it falling into the brooder!

Hang your lamp over one end of the brooder and adjust the height so it is about 95 degrees down where the chicks are hanging out.

Put your thermometer under the heat lamp on the shavings for a minute so you can see exactly what the temperature is there.

Putting the heat lamp all the way to one side of the brooder gives the chicks a place to go if they start to get too hot. They will just head down to the end without the lamp.

Every week lower the temperature about five degrees. The chicks will start to get their feathers during this time and will not need to be kept as warm. They will be fully feathered around eight weeks, and then they can move outside to their new home.

If your chicks are all huddled under the heat lamp, it's too cold for them and they are trying to gain warmth from each other. If they are all in a group at the far end away the heat lamp, it's likely too hot for them. If they are running all around the brooder and chirping away, it's just perfect!

Depending on the temperature outside, you can start taking your chicks out to play at about four weeks. Don't take them outside if it's really cold!

If you do take them out, keep a close eye on them. They tend to wander off quickly. And they can be really fast! If you have several chicks, take a sibling or a friend with you to help keep watch.

They will love exploring and learning about grass and scratching and all the other fun things chickens do! Now would be a good time to start naming them too!

How To Hold A Baby Chick

Hopefully you will want to hold your new chicks, check them out, play with them. That's awesome! They will love the time spent with you. We just need to make sure you know how to properly hold them.

This is definitely **not** the right way.

Your little chick could pop right out of your hands! And holding them so high off the ground is not safe either.

You want to make sure you have your chick secure and protected. Don't sneak up on your chicks either. No one likes being scared!

This is **perfect!** This sweet little chick is safe and secure. She won't fall out or jump out. She even fell asleep!

Make sure you don't hold too tight. Just a nice, loose, little cocoon is all she needs.

WARNING: Chicks poop. A lot. So don't be surprised if your chick poops on you while you are holding it.

Poop is part of raising chickens. You will have poop. Always wash your hands before you touch the chicks and afterwards too. Every time! You don't want to accidentally give them any germs or get any from them. So wash, wash, wash!

Is My Chicken A Girl Or A Boy?

Wouldn't it be wonderful if you could tell if your chick is a boy or a girl right when they are born? It would! With almost all breeds, you will not know if your chick is a boy or a girl for several weeks or maybe even months.

Being born with a pretty pink bow would make it easy!

Some breeds will keep you guessing a long time. Girl? Boy?

With other breeds, a few weeks are all you need to be fairly sure.

Certain breeds have something unique called an **auto sexing gene**. With these breeds, you will know right when they hatch if they are a girl or a boy. The girls will be a different color than the boys or have different markings.

If you hatch chicks, don't be surprised if you end up with more boys than girls. It seems to happen to everyone! Another mystery!

Moving Into The Coop

When your chicks are fully feathered, it's time to move them into their permanent home… their **chicken coop**! Chicken coops come in all shapes and sizes.

The important things to think about when deciding on a coop are:

- How many chickens will you have? Chickens need four square feet inside the coop. My experience has been that they don't actually need that much, but it's a good rule to go by. So if you think you might end up with six chickens, a coop that is 4 ft by 6 ft would be just about right.

- You will want a coop that is predator-proof. We will talk about that in a bit. Predators will always be something to consider when you have chickens.

- Your chickens will need either a protected **run** attached to their coop where they can go out and play, or you will need to let them **free range**. Free ranging is when they are let out of their coop to roam around freely outside. Most chickens love to free range, but you will need a place that has bushes, trees or some kind of cover they can run to in case of an unexpected predator. Enclosed chicken runs should have ten square feet per chicken.

A chicken run with a cover will keep out many predators. You will need to decide whether your flock can always have access to the run or if you will let them out each day.

- It's important that your coop have places where the chickens can get away from chilly winds. They will need a place to stay cozy and warm in the winter.

- Your coop will need proper **ventilation**. Ventilation is important so fresh air can get into the coop. There are different kinds of ventilation: windows, vents or covered openings. Ventilation is a must in your coop if you want to keep your chickens healthy.

Excessive heat can be deadly to chickens and good ventilation helps keep the coop cool. Most breeds can handle cold weather much better than hot.

Your chicken coop will need some kind of **ramp** for the chickens to use to get in and out of the coop.

A board with something for them to grip onto like this one works perfectly. You can also have a **pop door** that completely closes the opening.

We've already talked about nest boxes, and your new coop will need some of those. No need to have a bunch. Chickens will share! Plan to have one nest box for every 5-6 hens. Also be prepared to find eggs on the ground, outside, under a bush... those silly hens don't always follow the rules!

A nest box can be just about anything!

You will need to collect eggs every day. In the heat of a very hot summer, it's a good idea to do it more than once a day. Keep your nest box clean. Your hens will be happier and your eggs will be cleaner!

Hint: Fresh eggs will sink in a glass of water. If it floats, don't eat it!

Chickens don't sleep in beds like we do. They **roost** at night. A roost is an elevated wood board. You can use a 2 x 4 or a 4 x 4. You could even use a big branch!

Chickens like to roost in the highest point possible and will snuggle together to keep warm and for protection.

Your chickens will love having a roost or two in their coop!

When it starts to get dark and if they have access to their coop, your flock will go in for the night. You won't need to chase them or round them up at night. They do it all on their own!

Chicken coops come in all shapes and sizes. Use your imagination and find the perfect one for your family and flock! But plan ahead. There's a thing called chicken math that affects many chicken owners. Take the number of chickens you think you will have and then double or triple it!

Once you start keeping chickens, you will want more and more. You will see a breed you must have or fall in love with a special chicken a friend has available. If you hatch eggs from your hens, you will find it difficult to part with the chicks!

Taking Care Of Your Coop

One very important job you will have as a chicken owner is to take care of your coop. If your coop gets too dirty or if it gets wet, you might end up with a bunch of sick chickens. Tell your family that if they are eating the eggs, they can help with the cleaning!

Are you wondering why there aren't any pictures on this page? Because we are talking about dirty chicken coops! You don't want to see that, do you? Didn't think so. Now back to it...

At our farm, we use the **deep litter method**. It is the easiest way to keep your coop clean!

The deep litter method is where you let your coop litter build up over time. That's right! Don't clean it or change it. Told you it was easy!

As the chicken manure and litter compost (break down) inside the coop, it will help heat the coop and is very helpful with fly control. You might be wondering if it smells bad in there. Seems like it would, but it doesn't!

Here's how you do the deep litter method: Start by adding 4-6 inches of pine shavings in your coop. Toss or stir the litter every few days or weeks depending on much time your chickens spend in the coop and how many chickens you have. If the litter looks dirty, give it a toss!

We completely change out our litter (we use pine shavings) twice a year. Once all the litter is removed, thoroughly clean the inside of the coop with a water hose and get rid of cobwebs, poop, and anything else that shouldn't be there! Let it dry completely.

After the coop is dry, we use a mixture of ½ water and ½ white vinegar. Your mom probably has some in the kitchen. Put that mixture in a spray bottle and spray away! Get every little nook and cranny, the roosts, the nest boxes, everything. Let it dry and put in new litter.

Easy peasy!

Make sure to keep the old litter! Your parents will love to use it in their gardens! Don't use it for at least six months though. Before that, the litter can hurt the plants. Just pile it up somewhere and use it the next year. Chicken poop is super fertilizer!

VERY IMPORTANT!!! If you ever go into the coop and smell ammonia, drop everything and clean out your coop. The ammonia smells means the litter is wet somewhere and if your chickens breathe that in for any length of time, it can be deadly. Ask your parents for some ammonia so you can know what it smells like. Keeping the waterer outside will help but sometimes rain gets in through a window or crack. Never forget... no ammonia smell!

Predators Stay Away!

Unfortunately chickens have many predators that want to hurt them and part of your job is to keep them safe.

So who wants to harm this precious little chick?

Let's see. Raccoons, possums, dogs, cats, snakes, weasels, owls, coyotes, rats, foxes, skunks... and the worst... hawks.

Long list, isn't it?

So how can you help keep yours safe?

The best protection for your flock is a safe and secure chicken coop. If your flock free ranges during the day, make sure they have places to go for safety if a hawk flies overhead. Whenever I have lost a chicken during the day, it was to a hawk. Try to keep an eye on them while they are outside if possible.

If you do not have a very predator-proof attached chicken run, lock your chickens up at night so nothing can get in the coop. Make sure all doors are securely locked. If you have windows, cover them with hardware cloth.

Hardware cloth is vital to keeping chickens safe. It is much stronger than chicken wire and can be bought at your local hardware store. I highly recommend using it.

Most predators cannot rip through it so it is perfect to put over any opening that stays open on your coop. We never close our coop windows and have never had a problem with any predator getting in through a window.

This is what hardware cloth looks like. This guy knows he doesn't have to worry about predators!

We also put hardware cloth around the bottom of our chicken runs and up the sides about 8". Bend it at the bottom so part of it is on the grass outside the run, and then nothing will be able to dig under it either. The grass will grow right through it, and it won't be noticeable at all.

Make sure your coop does not have any cracks or openings. Some predators only need an inch or two to squeeze in. If you see anything, have someone help you patch it up.

Do your best to keep your coop safe. Your chickens will thank you for it!

Enjoy The Journey!

I hope you have enjoyed learning about keeping chickens and are ready to start! Every stage of raising your flock is enjoyable, educational and fun.

One day you are hatching eggs and suddenly you are collecting your very own eggs!

You might even start selling your eggs for money or begin your own breeding program selling hatching eggs and chicks to help other people get started. You might just decide to simply enjoy your new friends. So many possibilities once you get going!

Remember this: Every person who keeps chickens has their own unique way of doing it. I have been raising chickens for many years and have shared my knowledge and experience with you on these pages. You might do it differently, and that's fine too!

This book has tons of information in it. Reading it all at one time might be a bit overwhelming. Don't worry! Just take it one step at a time. You can do it!

Once you get your chicks, you have weeks to get the coop ready. Take each step as it comes and enjoy. Keeping chickens should be fun, and it is!

Good luck on your journey. I would love to hear from you about how you are doing, what breed you picked, and how much fun you are having with your new friends!

You can keep in touch with me at www.susanneblumer.com.

Now go start your flock!!

Glossary Of Terms

Air sac the pocket of air inside the big (round) part of the egg

Ameraucanas a pure breed of chicken that lays blue eggs

Auto Sexing Gene a gene that certain breeds carry that allow you to tell if the chick is a boy or girl at hatch time

Bantam the small version of a breed

Breed a certain type or kind of chicken

Brooder the first housing for newborn chicks

Broody a hen who wants to hatch eggs and stays in the nest box for long periods of time

Candling looking inside an egg with a bright light during the incubation period to determine if the chick is growing

Chick Feeder a feeder used with small chicks

Chick Starter the food used for chicks from birth to eight weeks old

Cock a male chicken over one year old

Cockerel a male chicken under one year old

Comb the growth on top of the chicken's head

Coop housing for chickens once they leave the brooder

Crow the sound a rooster makes

Deep Litter Method a method of composting litter in the coop

Dirt Bath the way chickens stay clean

Ear Lobes on the sides of the chickens face and come in different colors

Egg Tooth a small, sharp tooth chicks use to break through the shell when hatching

Egg Turner a part of the incubator that rotates the eggs back and forth

Flock a group of chickens

Free Range chickens that are allowed to roam freely instead of being confined to their coop

Grit gravel or small stones that chickens eat to help with digestion

Grower Feed the feed chicks need from eight weeks to 17 weeks

Hackles the feathers around the neck of the bird

Hatching   the process of hatching live chicks from fertilized eggs or the moment when the chick is born

Heat Lamp   a lamp used to keep chicks warm in the brooder

Hen   a female chicken that is older than one year

Humidity   the amount of moisture in the air in the incubator

Hygrometer   a small device that measures humidity

Incubator   a device used to hatch eggs

Incubation Period   the first 18 days of the hatch period

Layer Feed   the feed chickens eat after 17 weeks

Lockdown   the last three days of the incubation period and the time when the chicks hatch

Marans   a pure breed of chicken that lays very dark brown eggs

Molt   the yearly process of losing feathers

Nest Box   the place where the hen lays eggs

Pip   the initial break the chick makes in the egg while hatching

Pop Door   a small door on the coop that opens and closes and allows the chickens to go in and out of the coop

Predator   an animal that hunts other animals to harm or kill

Pullet   a female chicken that is less than a year old

Oliver Egger   a mixed breed of chicken that lays olive colored eggs

Ramp   a board that chickens walk on to get in and out of the coop

Roost   an elevated place in the coop where chickens sleep

Rooster   a male chicken that is over one year old

Run   an enclosed area attached to the coop where chickens

Saddle Feathers   the feathers just in front of the tail

Scratch   a grain mixture chickens eat

Standard   the large version of a breed

Temperature   how hot or cold it is in a certain place

Thermometer   the device that measures temperature

Ventilation   the replacement of stale air with fresh air

Waterer   something chicks and chickens drink from

Wattles   the red fleshy pieces that hang down under the beak

Zip   the process the chick takes to break open the egg while hatching

Additional information:

The website www.backyardchickens.com is a wonderful place to find answers, ask questions and meet other chicken owners in your area. Extremely informative.

Welp Hatchery and McMurray Hatchery are two excellent sources for baby chicks, geese, turkeys and ducks. You can find them on the internet.

A great incubator to start with is the Genesis 1588 HovaBator. As of printing time, this model was still being made. Occasionally, manufacturers will upgrade to a new model but keep most features the same. I use this exclusively during the lockdown period and do full hatches in it as well. There are so many options so do some research and see what works for you!

If you ever have a question or concern, Google is your friend! So many knowledgeable chicken keepers have shared their wisdom. Take advantage of it!

About The Author

Susanne Blumer lives on Huckleberry Farm in Upstate South Carolina with her husband Cole and two children, Colin & Annaliese. After moving to the farm, Susanne began breeding rare and heritage breed chickens. She sold hatching eggs to customers all over the country so they could get start their own flocks. Customers also drove from as far away as Miami and Ohio to purchase chicks and adult chickens. In addition to chickens, the farm is home to cows, donkeys, guineas, ducks, cats, Barbados sheep, miniature Babydoll sheep and three Great Pyrenees.

Susanne also has a series of Huckleberry Farm children's books and is the author of the upcoming Piper Periwinkle™ books. You can contact her at www.susanneblumer.com.

Made in the USA
Coppell, TX
08 March 2021

51436713R00043